LUKAS FOSS

The Jumping Frog
OF CALAVERAS COUNTY

Vocal Score

Libretto by
JEAN KARSAVINA
after a story
by MARK TWAIN

CARL FISCHER
INC.

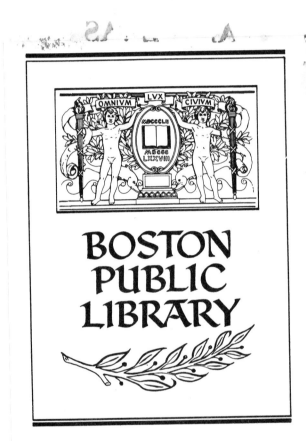

R.B.

LUKAS FOSS

The *Jumping Frog*

OF CALAVERAS COUNTY

Libretto by

JEAN KARSAVINA

after a story

by **MARK TWAIN**

Vocal Score

$7.50

Revised Edition

CARL FISCHER
INC.
62 Cooper Square, New York 10003
BOSTON • CHICAGO • DALLAS • LOS ANGELES

3720

Note

The performance of this opera or any part thereof, whether on stage, by radio, television, motion picture, mechanical reproduction or otherwise, and all other rights of any kind, nature or description, are controlled by Carl Fischer, Inc., and the use of said opera in any form or by any means is strictly prohibited unless written permission of Carl Fischer, Inc., is first obtained.

Reorchestrating or copying this opera in whole or in part by any means whatsoever and the use of any scores or parts not issued by the publisher are forbidden, and any such acts are subject to the penalties provided by the Copyright Law of the United States of America.

CARL FISCHER, INC.
56 Cooper Square
New York 3, N. Y.

Characters

Smiley	Tenor
1st Crapshooter	Tenor
2nd Crapshooter	Bass
Stranger	Bass
Lulu	Mezzo Soprano
Uncle Henry	Baritone
Guitar Player	Baritone
Optional Chorus	

THE STORY

The plot of *The Jumping Frog* is based on Mark Twain's well known tale, *The Celebrated Jumping Frog of Calaveras County*. The county is in California; the period is that of the Gold Rush. The curtain rises upon the inside of Uncle Henry's saloon. With him are Lulu (his niece) and Smiley, the proud owner of Daniel Webster, a frog locally noted for his prowess in jumping. Smiley reports that Dan'l has just jumped 14 feet and proclaims the frog a champion. To the admiration of Uncle Henry and Lulu, Smiley has Dan'l display his skill along the top of the counter at the bar. He then returns Dan'l to the box in which he is kept. The Stranger enters and orders a rye whiskey. He asks: "What might it be, you got in that box?" Smiley boasts to him about Dan'l. But the Stranger is unimpressed: "I don't see no p'ints 'bout that frog that's better'n any other frog." Smiley retorts: "I'll risk forty dollars that he outjumps any livin' frog in Calaveras County." The Stranger says that if he had a frog himself, he would take up the bet. Smiley undertakes to catch a frog for the Stranger. Each man deposits $40 with Uncle Henry. In a little quartet, the Stranger chuckles that he will fool Smiley, while the other three express their confidence in Dan'l. Smiley and Uncle Henry leave, the former to hunt a frog, the latter to "start the word goin' round 'bout that contest." While Lulu primps before a hand mirror, the Stranger notes a shotgun hanging on the wall near Dan'l's box and gets an idea. He says winningly to Lulu: "You wouldn't know where a lonesome man could find himself a square meal in this town, would you ma'am?" She replies: "I'm not a bad cook myself, they tell me." There is a brief interchange and Lulu leaves. The Stranger quickly takes buckshot out of the gun and stuffs it down Dan'l's throat. In a "grand" monologue, he boasts: "Each time I hit a town, I do the same; I shake a feller down and jump the blame. Find me a woman and give her the eye; then thank ye kindly ma'am and it's good-bye." He exults over his expected triumph. Scene II takes place in the village square, the saloon on one side and the general store on the other. Two men are shooting craps and a third sits on a railing strumming a guitar. They sing *Sweet Betsy from Pike*. Uncle Henry rushes in: "Save your money, gents . . . If you can bet on a sure thing, why risk your shirt?" He tells them about the wager and announces that the Stranger is welcoming side-bets. He says that the Stranger is coming in their direction together with Lulu. The three younger men, annoyed by her interest in the newcomer, declare that she will "gripe" when the Stranger is cleaned out and they win. Lulu and the Stranger arrive; the Crapshooters pretend to resume their game, while the Guitar Player picks up his guitar. The Stranger tells Lulu that the dinner was mighty good and was "served in real fine style." He wishes he could stay longer. Her wish agrees with his, "For you're my type of man," but she points out that, now that he knows the way, he can return frequently. The Crapshooters and the Guitar Player eavesdrop, and tease Lulu and the Stranger. The latter tells them that he knows that he's "chancin' an awful lot" to bet against Dan'l, but that "a gambler's got to gamble" and that he'll match their money if they want to bet. Lulu is afraid that he is too free with his cash and will not have any left "to buy a girl a present." Smiley rushes in with a frog for the Stranger. Uncle Henry calls out: "Make your bets! Come one! Come all!" Lulu feels uneasy; she hopes that she is going to favor the right side. The Stranger is confident; the faith of the other men in Dan'l is unshaken. Smiley and the Stranger prepare for the contest. It begins with the Stranger's frog making a small jump; Dan'l is planted as solid as a church. Smiley, Uncle Henry, the Crapshooters and the Guitar Player plead with Dan'l to jump, but nothing happens. Lulu, moved by old-time loyalty, whispers: "Don't let 'em down, Dan'l." But Dan'l collapses. The Stranger collects all the money, gives $20 to Lulu, and, amid the lamentations of the other men over the defeat of Dan'l, quietly leaves. The group begins to disperse. Suddenly Smiley calls out: "Hey, look it!" and points out that Dan'l isn't feeling well. Smiley picks up Dan'l, says he weighs five pounds, and turns him upside down. Dan'l vomits up the buckshot. The Crapshooters rush off to capture the Stranger and come back pushing and manhandling him. They shake him until they recover all the money and, after threatening to tar and feather him if he ever returns, run him out of town. There is no longer any doubt as to Lulu's sentiments. Everybody sings the praises of Daniel the Frog, and Smiley is borne in triumph on the shoulders of the Guitar Player and Crapshooters as the curtain falls.

To Ellie

The Jumping Frog of Calaveras County

Libretto by
JEAN KARSAVINA
after a story by
MARK TWAIN

Music by
LUKAS FOSS

OVERTURE

1) Orchestra Score and Parts on rental.

Duration
45 minutes

sempre stacc.
cresc.
ff
dolce
p
etc.
sempre stacc.
cresc.
f
mp

f
mp
p dolce
dim.
pp
f
p
pp
f
p
pp
pp

sempre pp
mf
sf
sf
pp
p
cresc.

p cresc.
ff
8
dolce
p
etc.
sempre stacc.
cresc.
poco
f
mp
f
mp
p dolce

dim.
pp
sonore
p
sonore
p
sonore
p
sonore
pp
leggiero

p cresc.
sempre stacc.
mf cresc.
8
f cresc.
marcato
sf
sf
ff
R.H. 5
10
L.H.
15
sf
sf

SCENE I

Uncle Henry's Bar in Calaveras. The decor is typical of the Gold Rush days, Calaveras being half town, half camp.

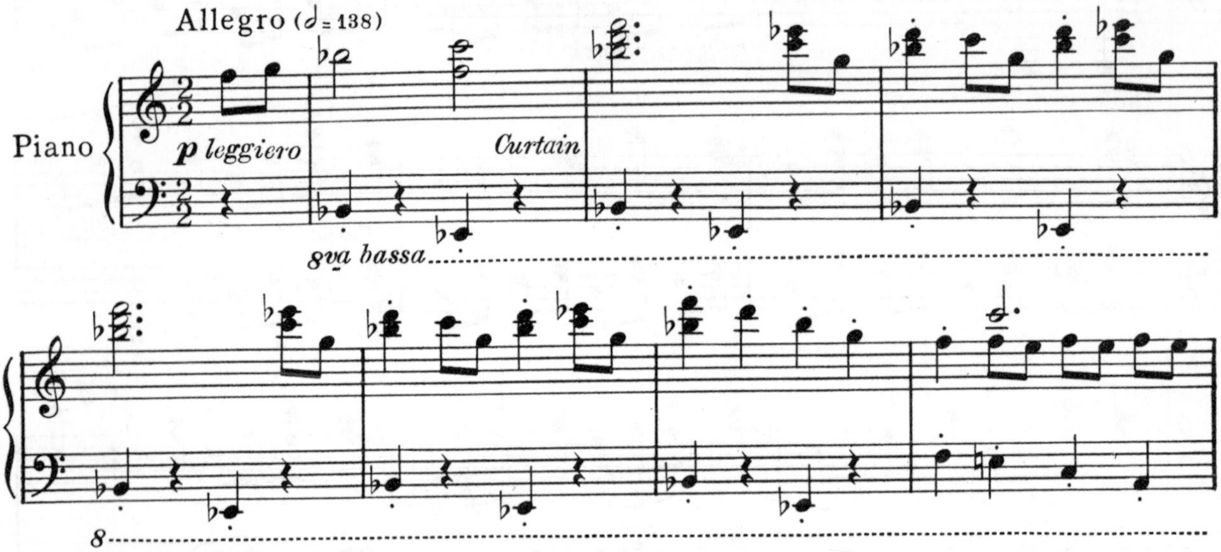

Uncle Henry is bar-tending. Smiley and Miss Lulu are at the counter.

to Uncle Henry
mf
p
Sm.
it's the truth. My Dan-l's a cham-pion,
R.H.
sf
p
to Lulu
a cham-pion!
Jumped four-teen feet, caught
pp legg.
poco a poco cresc.
poco
four-teen flies! Who'd be-lieve a var-mint his size, a

Lu.
Sm.
U.H.
espr.
coun - try frog,
Uncle Henry (who's been pouring drinks) mf
Here's to Dan - 'l
mf
To Dan - 'l
To
cresc.
4
the jump - ing cham-pion,
to Dan - 'l!
Here's to
espr.
a coun - try frog!
Dan - 'l
the jump - ing frog!
f
Here's to
Dan - iel the frog,
the
Dan - iel the frog,
the jump-ing frog,
8

5
Lu.
— the jump - ing frog of Cal - a - ve - ras Coun - ty!
Sm.
jump - ing frog — of Cal - a - ve - ras Coun - ty!
U.H.
— the jump - ing frog of Cal - a - ve - ras Coun - ty!
8
mp
Dan - 'l Web - ster will make us fa - mous,
p
p
6
Put us all on the map he will! —
If we brag a bit, who can blame us?
p

U.H.
Ain't man-y frogs with his jump - ing skill, — not
mp
U.H.
7
man-y frogs! ————
p
f
Lu.
f
Here's to Dan-'l ————
Sm.
f
Here's to Dan-'l ———— the jump-ing frog, the
U.H.
f
Here's to Dan-'l ———— the jump-ing frog, ————
3

8
Lu.
— the jump - ing frog of Cal - a - ve - ras Coun - ty!
Sm.
jump - ing frog ——— of Cal - a - ve - ras Coun - ty!
U.H.
— the jump - ing frog of Cal - a - ve - ras Coun - ty!
mp
Lu.
Dan - 'l Web - ster is smart, you said it,
p
Lu.
Does what no oth - er frog can do, —— But
9
pp

Lu.
Smi - ley here — de - serves some cred - it, We
p
Lu.
mf
10
aim to brag, — we aim to brag, we aim to brag on Smi - ley too. —
mf
p
f sub.
Lu.
f
Here's to Smi - ley — who trained the frog, —
Sm.
f
To Dan-'l the jump - ing
U.H.
f
Here's to Smi - ley who trained the jump - ing frog, who

Lu.
Sm.
U.H.
frog, the jump-ing frog, the jump-ing
trained the jump-ing frog, who trained the jump-ing frog, who
11
the jump-ing frog of Cal - a-ve-ras Coun-ty! To Smi-ley!
frog, the jump-ing frog of Cal - a-ve-ras Coun-ty! To
trained the jump-ing frog of Cal-a-ve-ras Coun-ty! To Smi-ley!
p
f
To Smi-ley! Here's to you!
lifting a hand modestly.
poco rit.
Dan-'l! To Dan-'l! I ain't
To Smi-ley! Here's to you!
sf
poco rit.

12
a tempo
p cantabile
Sm.
done much, learned him pa - tient, learned him pa - tient -
p legg.
a tempo
Sm.
like and slow; All a frog wants is an ed-u-
13
poco rit. p
Sm.
ca - tion, And he'll learn what he has to
pp
poco rit.
p
dolce
a tempo
pp leggiero
Lu.
Our Smi - ley, we de-clare, is the best in
pp
Sm.
know,
pp leggiero
U.H.
Our Smi - ley, we de-clare, is the best in
pp a tempo

14
Lu.
Cal - a - ve - ras. Our Smi - ley, we de - clare, is the best in Cal - a - ve - ras,
Sm.
U.H.
Cal - a - ve - ras. Our Smi - ley, we de - clare, is the best in Cal - a - ve - ras,
Lu.
the best in Cal - a - ve - ras, and that's a fact.
Sm.
U.H.
the best in Cal - a - ve - ras, and that's a fact.
sf
Poco meno mosso
15
Sm.
espr.
And he'll learn what he has to
U.H.
espr.
And he'll learn what he has to
p legato

Tempo I
espr.
pp
Lu.
And he'll learn what he has to know.
Sm.
know, what he has to know. I on-ly learned him pa-tient,
UH.
know, what he has to know.
poco rit.
p
16
marc.
I don't know when I seen
gave him an ed-u-ca-tion, I on-ly learned him pa-tient, gave him an
U.H.
I don't know when I seen
cresc.
an-y-bod-y smart-er, when I seen an-y-bod-y smart-er, and that's a
ed-u-ca-tion, gave him an ed-u-ca-tion, and that's a
an-y-bod-y smart-er, when I seen an-y-bod-y smart-er, and that's a

17
p cresc.
Lu.
fact.
p cresc.
Sm.
fact.
mf
U.H.
fact. Well I de - clare, well I de-
p
Lu.
f
To Smi-ley!
mf
Well I de -
Sm.
mf
Well I de - clare,
U.H.
f
clare, I nev-er seen a man so clev-er.
8
8
p

Lu.
clare, well I de - clare, I
Sm.
well I de - clare, I ain't done
8
18
f
Lu.
nev-er seen,
pp
I de-clare, I nev-er
Sm.
much,
mp
There sure was nev - er a frog so
U.H.
f
To Smi-ley!
pp
I de - clare, I nev-er seen a
8
sf
p

Lu.
seen a man so clev - er, I de-clare, I nev - er
Sm.
clev - er, there sure was nev - er a frog so
U.H.
man so clev - er, I de - clare, I nev - er seen a
cresc.
Lu.
seen a man so clev - er, seen a man so clev - er,
cresc.
Sm.
clev - er, a frog so clev - er, a frog so
cresc.
U.H.
man so clev - er, seen a man so clev - er, a
cresc.

Lu.
a man so clev - er, so clev - er!
Sm.
clev - er, a frog so clev - er!
U.H.
man so clev - er, a man so clev - er!
sf
ff poco rubato
19
Sm.
Come on, Dan - iel, let's show these folks!
p
Daniel is taken out of his box (in pantomime).
(No physical representation of a frog need appear.)
mf

20
DANIEL'S DANCE
Doppio lento (Andantino) (𝅗𝅥 = 69)
p
21
espr.
dim. e rit.
espr.
Allegro (𝅗𝅥 = 138)
Lu.
Sm.
U.H.
pp
Our Dan-'l, we de-clare, is the best in Cal-a-ve-ras,
Our Dan-'l, we de-clare, is the best in Cal-a-ve-ras,
Our Dan-'l, we de-clare, is the best in Cal-a-ve-ras,
pp

22
Lu.
our Dan-'l, we de-clare, is the best in Cal-a-ve - ras, the best in
Sm.
our Dan-'l, we de-clare, is the best in Cal-a-ve - ras, the best in
U.H.
our Dan-'l, we de-clare, is so mod-est, so straight-for-ward, so mod-est,
cresc.
f
Cal-a-ve - ras, and that's a fact!
Cal-a-ve - ras, and that's a fact!
so straight-for -ward, and that's a fact! Well I de - clare,
p cresc.
mf
23
To Dan-'l!
Well I de-
well I de - clare, I nev-er seen a frog so

Lu.
Well I de - clare, well I de - clare, I
Sm.
clare, I nev-er seen a frog so
U.H.
clev-er!
Lu.
nev-er seen, I de-clare, I nev-er
Sm.
clev-er! There sure was nev - er a frog so
U.H.
To Dan-'l! I de - clare, I nev-er seen a

24
Lu.
seen a frog so clev - er, I de - clare, I nev - er
Sm.
clev - er, there sure was nev - er a frog so
U.H.
frog so clev - er, I de - clare, I nev - er seen a
8
Lu.
cresc.
seen a frog so clev - er, seen a frog so clev - er,
Sm.
cresc.
clev - er, a frog so clev - er, a frog so
U.H.
cresc.
frog so clev - er, seen a frog so clev - er, a
8
cresc.

Lu.
a frog so clev - er, so clev - er!
Sm.
clev - er, a frog so clev - er!
U.H.
frog so clev-er, a frog so clev - er!
8
sf p sub.
ff poco rubato
3
Come on, Dan-iel, you can do bet-ter than that!
25
sempre p
cresc.
molto cresc.
Daniel resumes his demonstration.
Doppio lento
ff sost.

pp
p
pp
26
The biggest leap
pp
poco
rit.
ppp
Doppio mosso
U.H.
p leggiero
He is the
pp
p leggiero
U.H.
He offers a drink to Dan'l.
27
cham-pion!
A drink to him, he de-serves it.

leggiero
U.H.
There's no-one like him in all of Cal-a - ve-ras
espress.
28
Lu.
In all of Cal - a - ve - ras Coun-ty,
Sm.
p
In all of Cal-a - ve - ras, in all of Cal - a - ve-ras
U.H.
Coun - ty, in all of Cal - a - ve - ras!
p
Lu.
in all of Cal - a - ve - ras,
espress.
Sm.
Coun-ty, Cal - a - ve - ras,
mf
U.H.
Was ev - er frog so rare as the pride of Cal - a - ve - ras,

legg.
29
cresc.
Lu.
the jump-ing frog, the jump-ing frog! Was ev-er
Sm.
legg.
Was ev-er frog so rare as the pride of Cal-a-ve-ras, the jump-ing
espr.
U.H.
Cal - a - ve - ras,
cresc.
Lu.
frog so rare as the pride of Cal-a-ve-ras, the pride of Cal-a-
Sm.
fp
frog, the jump-ing frog, the jump-ing frog
legg.
U.H.
the jump-ing frog, the jump-ing frog, the jump-ing
30
Lu.
ff
ve-ras Coun-ty? To Dan-'l! To Dan the jump-ing frog—
Sm.
ff
of Cal-a-ve-ras Coun-ty? To Dan-'l! To Dan-'l,
U.H.
ff
frog of Cal-a-ve-ras Coun-ty? To Dan-'l! To Dan-'l,

Lu.
of Cal-a-ve-ras Coun-ty!
Sm.
the jump-ing frog of Cal-a-ve-ras Coun-ty!
U.H.
the jump-ing frog of Cal-a-ve-ras Coun-ty!
sf
ff poco con moto
Smiley puts the frog back in the box.
Uncle Henry has filled up the glasses and they all drink up.
31
non rit.
32
Enter Stranger.
Andantino (♩ = 92)
pp
mf
pp
pp

accel.
a tempo
poco f
33
Faster
Andantino
U.H.
Not at all, Stranger, make yourself to home.
Slow
Stranger (in a deep, ominous tone)
Str.
Mind if I join you?
Thank you.
p
dolce (ma non espr.)
Str.
Rhy whis-key.
p
poco moto
legg.
rit.
Sm.
(pretending casual indifference.)
34
a tempo
Str.
Might be a
What might it be you got in that box?
a tempo
pp

Sm.
par-rot, might be a ca-na-ry but it ain't, Stran-ger, it's on-ly
Sm.
just a frog.
Con moto (♩ = 116)
Str.
A frog?
sf
mf
p
Str.
Well of all things!
35
A frog be-longs in a bog!
mf
p
Sm.
Not this one, not Dan-iel.
He's spe-cial, he's tal-ent-ed.
legato

Stranger laughs loudly.
Sm.
He's Dan-'l Web-ster, pride of our coun-ty.
cresc.
f
p with mean irony.
36
Str.
I heard of pet cats and roos-ters And rats and seals and
p
Str.
ped-i-greed hogs, There's ma-ny
pp
Falsetto
37
Str.
con-tend a dog's man's best friend, But who ev-er keeps pet
p

Sm.
mf
cresc.
f accel.
Some not on-ly keep 'em, some train 'em.
Str.
frogs?
pp
cresc.
accel.
Stranger laughs again.
38
f
I seen a trained pig start danc-ing a jig,
SILENT
mp a tempo stacc.
Lu.
p
Lis-ten to him mockin' Dan! Ain't he just the mean-est
Sm.
p
Lis-ten to him mockin' Dan! Ain't he just the mean-est
U.H.
p
Lis-ten to him mockin' Dan! Ain't he just the mean-est
Str.
I seen a trained flea.
pp

Lu.
Sm.
U.H.
Str.
man?
man?
man?
f
p
Falsetto
And once at the zoo a trained kan-ga-roo, but a trained frog
8
mf
p
p
39
Più mosso (Allegro) (𝅗𝅥 = 112)
p legg.
Lis-ten to him,
p legg.
Lis-ten to him,
p legg.
Lis-ten to him,
I nev-er did see!
pp

Lu.
lis - ten to him, lis - ten to him, lis - ten to him, lis - ten to him!
Sm.
lis - ten to him, lis - ten to him, lis - ten to him, lis - ten to him!
U.H.
lis - ten to him, lis - ten to him, lis - ten to him, lis - ten to him!
mp
Lu.
Stran - ger, hard - ly come to
Sm.
mp
U.H.
Stran - ger, hard - ly come to town,
To Smiley.
f
Str.
Well, what can he do?

40
Lu.
town, Stran - ger runs our Dan - 'l down!
Sm.
to Stranger
Do? Let's see...
U.H.
tries to run our Dan - 'l down!
Sm.
excited
p
Give 'em a lit - tle punch and he'll start to whirl, whirl in the air like a
p
Sm.
dough - nut. Give 'em an - oth - er punch and he'll sum - mer - set,
f
p

41
Sm.
pp
land on his feet too, sure as a cat. Catch an - oth - er fly
3
3
pp
mp
poco rit.
'fore you say scat. Then with his hind - foot in - dif - f'rent - like, he'll
p
poco rubato
p espr.
3
3
fall to scratch - in' his head, to scratch - in' his side, not proud at
p meno mosso
p
all. Like what he just done?
42 Andantino (𝅗𝅥 = 69)
p

Sm.
Str.
Noth - ing but the pur - est fun.
mp in a low monotone, with utter contempt
Nope, I don't see no p'ints 'bout that frog that's bet-ter'n an - y oth - er frog!
p
deeply wounded
May-be you don't, Stran-ger.
poco string.
cresc.
May-be you've no ex - pe-rience. May-be as
sfp
cresc.

43
Sm.
f
p
𝅗𝅥 = 84
molto espr.
frogs go you're just an am - a-chure, but I got my o -
dolce cresc.
pin - ion, and one thing is
string.
44
f poco rubato
sure, I'll risk for - ty dol - lars
sf
Vivace (𝅗𝅥 = 126)
ff poco sostenuto

poco rubato
ff
Sm.
that he out - jumps an - y liv - in' frog in Cal - a - ve - ras Coun - ty!
Stranger
Andantino (♩ = 92)
45
Str.
p
I'm just a stran - ger here. I got no frog,
string.
sf
p
Str.
but if I had a frog, I'd bet you.
rit.
8
Smiley
con moto
Sm.
p
Seems hard - ly fair to let you, still,
Più mosso (𝅗𝅥 = 104)
pp
8

1) Stage money must be gold coins.

f espr.
47
Lu.
With-out a doubt he'll win this bout! He'll
Sm.
crowd him out! He'll win hands
U.H.
espr.
this bout! He'll win this bout, he'll
Str.
frog. I'll find a way to fool them all,
mf
Lu.
win hands down the cham-pion's crown! To Dan-'l! He'll
Sm.
down the cham - pion's crown! To Dan-'l! He'll
U.H.
win hands down the cham-pion's crown! To Dan-'l! He'll
Str.
I bet their frog won't jump at all! They think I'm
8

Lu.
Sm.
U.H.
Str.
win the match, beat an-y frog that you can catch!
win the match, beat an-y frog that you can catch! He'll
win — the match, he'll win the match, beat an-y frog that you can catch!
just a gam - bling fool, To trust a frog from an-y pool!
p
tr
espr.
Make us fa -
poco dolce
win the race — and prove our case, Make us fa -
Make us fa -
p leggiero
The stu - pid dupes, the nin - com - poops,
p sub.
espr.
p sempre

48
Lu.
- - mous, if we brag,
Sm
leggiero
- - mous, if we brag, and if we brag,
U.H.
- - mous, if we brag,
Str
The dirt-y duds, the stick-in-the-
p
Lu.
espr.
p
f
who can blame us? To
Sm
espr.
p
f
who can blame us? To
U.H.
espr.
p
f
who can blame us? To
Str
aside
mp
muds, I bet their frog won't jump at all!
p

Lu.
Sm.
U.H.
Str.
Dan-iel!
To
Dan-iel!
To
Dan-iel!
To
I'll find a way to fool them all!
sf
p
49
Dan-iel!
Dan-iel!
Dan-iel!
pp
p a tempo
They think I'm just an
sf
p poco rit.
dim.
ppp a tempo
sf

Sm.
A
U.H.
A
Str.
am - a - chure, Their brag - gin' is pre - ma - ture,
Lu.
He'll win the race and prove our
Sm.
jump - ing match! A jump - ing match!
U.H.
jump - ing match! He'll win the race!
Str.
I'll find a way to fool 'em all, I bet their frog won't jump at
pp
mp espr.
mf
mp
legg.
tr

50
Lu.
Sm.
U.H.
Str.
p sub.
case, he'll win!
He'll win!
He'll win!
all! I'll fool them all, I'll fool them all, I'll
fool them all!
p
poco
pp
con delicatezza

dim.
pp
mp
51
U.H.
Guess we better start the word goin' 'round 'bout that contest.
poco marc.
mp
Uncle Henry puts box with Daniel on the counter.
Stranger sees shotgun and next to it the box with Daniel.
He gets an idea.
Andante (♩= 84)
U.H.
You go tell the boys in the backroom, Lulu.
Uncle Henry exits.
Smiley exits.
pp
non leg.
Lulu takes out a large hand mirror from her reticule and starts primping.
Stranger
Andante quasi adagio
(slyly) poco rubato
Str.
He approaches Lulu.
You would-n't know where a
molto accel.
poco cresc.
sf
p

52
Lento
Str.
lone-some man could find him-self a square meal in this town, would you, Ma'am?
pp
Allegro
Andante
Lu.
I'm not a bad cook my-self, they tell me.
Str.
Why, Ma'am, I
pp
rit.
non leg.
Più lento
Lu.
I got a soft heart! Nev-er could stand the thought of a
Str.
did-n't mean...
p dolce

Presto
Lulu exits.
Lu.
lone-some man! You jus' wait here.
Stranger walks slowly in the direction of Daniel's box.
pp
lento
pp
Andante sostenuto
ff
Stranger climbs on the counter to reach the shotgun hung up above.
Vivace (𝅗𝅥 = 92)
Stranger takes buck-shot out of the gun.
He rushes towards Daniel's box.
lunga
He takes Daniel out, pries open the frog's jaws. With a broad wink at the audience he stuffs Dan'l with buckshot.
lento
pp
He puts Daniel back in the box.

Stranger relaxes, grins broadly, pours himself some whiskey

55
sostenuto
Str.
this time, by gol-ly, I'm hav-in' me the works.
Più mosso (𝅗𝅥 = 92)
56
Tempo I (♩ = 69)
Stranger
Più mosso (♩ = 92)
Str.
Each time I hit a town, turn on the

Str.
charm, I do my-self some good, so where the hell's the harm?
57
Str.
If a wo-man likes me, we have us a time;
Str.
Let her feed and love me, now where's the crime? Each time, each
rit.
Più mosso (𝅗𝅥 = 92)
Str.
time, each time, each time I cheat them, then hit the trail,
gliss.
R.H.

58
Str.
Know how to treat them and stay out of jail. —
With an ace in the hole,
gliss.
sfp
mf
p
why play it straight?
When they find me out they're al-ways too late, they're al-ways
f
59
too late!
Each
♩ = 69
rit.
Tempo I (♩ = 69)
time I'm on the make,
I
fool
these
bums,
I

Str.
take a-way the cake and leave 'em the crumbs! _
pochiss. con moto
Just keep on the look-out _ for the big chance, _
60
cresc.
poco più mosso
When it comes grab it by the seat of the pants. Each
poco rit.
f poco rit.
♩ = 69
molto rit.
time, each time I fool 'em, _ Take what they
♩ = 92
f molto rit.

61
pp
Str.
got, But this time, by gol-ly, I hit the
3
8
Vivace (𝅗𝅥 = 126)
ff
jack - pot! For-ty dol-lars U. S.
pp cresc.
ff p sub
shout all high notes
mon-ey and a home cooked meal;
62
Lov-in' with-out mat-ri-mo-ny, an all-round good

Str.
deal! For-ty dol-lars U. S. mon-ey,
fp
Str.
that's a good day's haul,
fp
fp
Str.
Grab it up and kiss my hon-ey, and good-bye
63
sfp
ff
shouted
Str.
all!
8
p cresc.
f
sff
8

SCENE II

The village square. This is where the two streets of Calaveras cross, forming the center for the life of the town. Catty corner from each other, the bar and the general store. The store has a wooden porch with a railing. Two men are shooting crap on the porch floor while a third sits on the railing strumming a guitar. All three wear frontier clothes. Before curtain someone on stage is whistling "Sweet Betsy" with the orchestra.

G. Pl.
mountains with her lover Ike, With two yokes of oxen and
one spotted hog, An old Shanghai rooster and an old yellow
3
1st Crapshooter
1st Cr.
mf
So roll, you old bones, roll along, roll a-
G. Pl.
dog.
2nd Crapshooter
2nd Cr.
mf
So roll, you old bones, roll along, roll a-
CHORUS (Optional)
TENORS
T
mf
So roll, you old bones, roll along, roll a-
BASSES
B
mf
So roll, you old bones, roll along, roll a-
mp
3
3
3

1st Cr.
long, May - be you'll do bet - ter if
G.Pl.
You'll do bet - ter if
2nd Cr.
long, May - be you'll do bet - ter if
T
long, May - be you'll do bet - ter if
B
long, May - be you'll do bet - ter if
cresc.
4
1st Cr.
I sing a song.
G.Pl.
I sing a song.
2nd Cr.
I sing a song.
T
I sing a song.
B
I sing a song.
f
dim.

G.Pl.
p
Now Bet - sy and Ike reached Cal - i - for - ni -
p
8
ay, They liked what they saw, said we think that we'll
8
8
5
stay. We'll stake us a claim, go pros - pect - in' for
8
gold, And may - be we'll strike some be - fore we grow
8

⑥
1st Cr.
G.Pl.
2nd Cr.
T
B
f
old. So roll, you old bones, roll a - long, roll a -
long, May - be you'll do bet - ter if

1st Cr.
I sing a song.
G.Pl.
I sing a song.
2nd Cr.
I sing a song.
T
I sing a song.
B
I sing a song.
sf
SILENT
7
mp
The coun-try's wide o-pen, there's rich-es e-
p
nough, The wo-men are few and the men they are rough, And

8
1st Cr.
may - be you'll stay rich and may - be you'll not,
p legg.
1st Cr.
a tempo
And gam-blin's a
pp poco rit.
p a tempo
9
1st Cr.
sure way to lose what you got.

10
1st Cr.
mf
Roll a - long, you old bones,
G.Pl.
mf
Roll a - long, you old bones,
2nd Cr.
ff
Come sev-en, come e-lev-en, my pile's get - tin' low,
TENORS
T
mf
Roll a - long, you old bones,
1st BASSES
B
mf
Roll a - long, you old bones,
2nd BASSES
B
mf
Come sev-en, come e-lev-en, his pile's get - tin' low,
f non leg.
1st Cr.
roll a - long, roll a - long,
G.Pl.
roll a - long, roll a - long, May -
2nd Cr.
If I had sense I'd be quit - tin' right now, My hunch-es are wrong, and I'm
T
roll a - long, roll a - long,
B
roll a - long, roll a - long, May -
B
If he had sense he'd be quit - tin' right now, His hunch-es are wrong, and he's

Uncle Henry comes rushing in.
1st Cr.
if I sing you a song.
U.H.
Save
G.Pl.
be you'll do bet - ter if I sing you a song.
2nd Cr.
down on my luck, And if I win now I'll be plumb thun-der-struck.
T
if I sing you a song.
B
be you'll do bet - ter if I sing you a song.
B
down on his luck, And if he wins now I'll be plumb thun-der-struck.
sf
Allegro (𝅗𝅥 = 126-132)
f
11
U.H.
your lu - cre, gents, Hold on to your pay-dirt. If you can
3
sf
sf

1st Cr.
U.H.
G.Pl.
2nd Cr.
What's — the good word?
bet on a sure thing, why risk your shirt?
What's on, — Hen-ry?
What's the good word?
12
What's the prop-o - si - tion?
Ain't you heard? —
What's the prop-o-si -tion?
What's the prop-o - si - tion?

p
dim.
sf
mf
U.H.
Damn fool stran-ger comes in
13
leggiero
my sa-loon, takes a look at Smi-ley, takes a look at Dan-'l.
Nope, he says, there's noth-in' 'bout that frog that's

high, off pitch
14
1st Cr.
That
U.H.
bet-ter'n an-y oth-er frog.
G.Pl.
Nev-er heard the like!
2nd Cr.
I'll be dog - gone!
1st Cr.
stran-ger don't have the sense he was born with.
mp dim.
U.H.
And right-a-way he bets for-ty dol-lars,
pp

15
U.H.
says an-y oth-er frog can out-jump 'im, and that ain't all,
f
U.H.
and that ain't all, for he hol-lers side bets are wel-come.
f
16
p leggiero
1st Cr.
Crazy fool! Bet you can't guess who my mon-ey's on, bet you
mf
U.H.
We'll stump 'im! We'll
G. Pl.
We'll show him! Bet you
2nd Cr.
We'll teach him a lesson!
p
poco cresc.

1st Cr.
can't guess who my mon-ey's on, bet you can't guess who my mon-ey's on.
U.H.
stump 'im! We'll stump 'im!
G.Pl.
can't guess who my mon-ey's on, bet you can't guess who my mon-ey's on.
2nd Cr.
Bet you can't guess who my mon-ey's on.
U.H.
Eas - y! He'll be com-in' soon, he'll
p sub. e leggiero
U.H.
be here an - y min-ute now; we'll hold that con - test
17

1st Cr.
I'm ready - y
U.H.
here. Eas - y! You have - n't heard the
G.Pl.
We'll stump 'im all right!
2nd Cr.
Hoo - ray!
U.H.
best yet. Fact is, he's com - in' with Lu - lu.
as if whispering

High off pitch
18
1st Cr.
That stranger don't have the sense he was born with.
G.Pl.
I'll be dog-gone! That girl comes high,
2nd Cr.
I'll be dog-gone!
p sub.
nasty
She'll start to gripe
then she'd like to spit in your eye if you're not her type.
19
when he's cleaned out.
She will!
You said it!
She will!

1st Cr.
2nd Cr.
I'll be dog-gone if she don't!
When he's cleaned out!
U.H.
Feller must be a city slicker but as frogs go he's sure
When we win out
cresc.
sempre stacc.
to Uncle Henry
Maybe it was the licker.
no picker.
G.Pl.
mf cresc.
20
When we win out
the jump - ing bout
cresc. poco a poco

1st Cr.
U.H.
G.Pl.
2nd Cr.
f cresc.
We'll sure win
f to 1st Crapshooter
Nope, he was cold-stone sober.
with - out a doubt.
with - out a doubt.
deep, in front of stage
ff
I'll be dog -
out. It's Dan-'l Web - ster our mon - ey's on, it's
It's Dan-'l Web - ster our mon - ey's on, it's
gone! It's Dan-'l Web - ster our mon - ey's on, it's
TENORS
T
BASSES
B
poco rit.
ff a tempo

21
1st Cr.
Dan-'l Web-ster our mon-ey's on, it's Dan-'l, it's
U.H.
Dan-'l Web-ster our mon-ey's on, it's Dan-'l, it's
G.Pl.
Dan-'l Web-ster our mon-ey's on, it's Dan-'l, it's
2nd Cr.
Dan-'l Web-ster our mon-ey's on, it's Dan-'l, it's
T
Dan-'l Web-ster our mon-ey's on, it's Dan-'l, it's
B
Dan-'l Web-ster our mon-ey's on, it's Dan-'l, it's
1st Cr.
Dan-'l, Dan-'l.
U.H.
ff
Dan-'l, Dan-'l. Sh
G.Pl.
Dan-'l, Dan-'l.
2nd Cr.
Dan-'l, Dan-'l.
T
Dan-'l, Dan-'l.
B
Dan-'l, Dan-'l.
ff

U.H.
p
3
There they are!
22
8
3
p legg.
3
pp
They turn their backs to Stranger and Lulu, who enter arm in arm.
Crapshooters resume their game, apparently. Guitar Player picks up his guitar.
Andante maestoso (♩=88)
Stranger (hammy)
Str.
That was a might - y good din - ner, And
p
sotto voce
23 With mocking sentimentality
Str.
served in re - al fine style, And you were a
(ree - yul)
dolce
p sub.
espr.
Str.
re - al won - der - ful host - ess, Wish I was stay - in' a -
pp
p

Snicker in the background.
Allegretto (♩ = 176)
Str.
while.
24
pp leggiero
poco string.
Pochiss. sost. ma allegretto
p
L'istesso Tempo (Allegretto)
mf dead pan voice
25
Lu.
Wish you could stay a lot long-er,
Lu.
For you're my type of man, But
sempre stacc.

26
Lu.
cresc.
p
p espr.
now you know the way, Hon-ey, You can come a-gain and a-
poco cresc.
p
Andante (♩= 92)
gain.
Str.
mf
That's re-al big of you, Sug-ar, I
pp
p legato
hope you mean what you say, For I'll take you
27
pp
up on that prop-o-si-tion When-ev-er I trav-el this
espr.

Più mosso (𝅗𝅥 = 90)
f agitato
Lu.
Must you go, Hon - ey?
Str.
way.
f
'Fraid I have to.
f sub.
mf
f
28
f sempre agitato
Lu.
Can't you set - tle down a - while?
mp
dim.
mf
Str.
p
poco rit.
I'm a roll - ing stone, a roll - ing stone by na - ture,
p
pp sub.
poco rit.
mf
29
Str.
set - tlin' down ain't my style.
mf
dim.
p
3
rit.
3
3

Andante (♩= 92)
Lu.
Str.
p
Wish you could stay a lot long - er, For
Wish I could stay a lot long - er, We're
your my type of man,
tak - in' just what we can,
30
espr.
No use cry - in',
No use ly - in',

Lu.
rit.
May - be I'll meet you, may - be I'll meet you a -
Str.
rit.
May - be I'll meet you, meet you a -
rit.
f

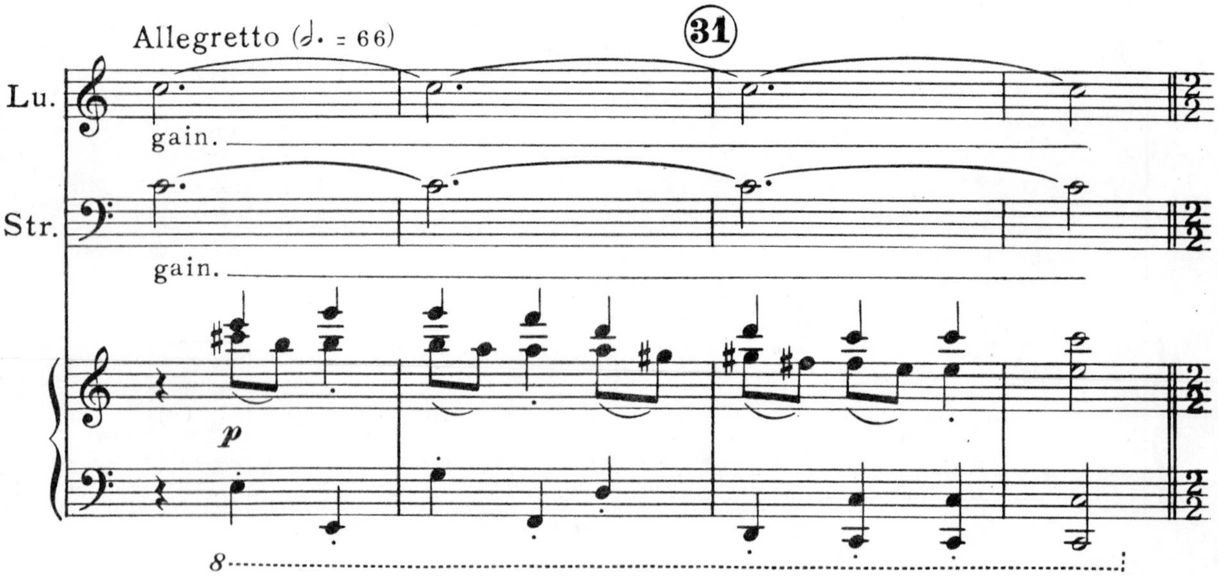
Allegretto (♩. = 66)
31
Lu.
gain.
Str.
gain.
p
8

General applause from the onlookers.
Then shouts ad lib. "Howdy!" "Howdy!" "How you been."

Allegro (𝅗𝅥 = 132)
Str.
Howdy, Uncle Henry, Howdy. Howdy, everybody!
f

Lu.
2nd Crapshooter
2nd Cr.
mp
How you been, Lu - lu?
Miss - s - s - s - s
p legg.
32
Lu - lu to you!
1st Crapshooter
1st Cr.
'Fore you get high and might - y,
bet - ter wait till the con - test's through,
bet - ter wait,
bet - ter wait.
U.H.
Bet - ter wait.
G. Pl.
Bet - ter wait.
Bet - ter wait till the con - test's through.
Str.
Folks,
cresc.

33
poco rubato
Str.
I know what you're think-ing,
ff
p
Str.
I'm chanc-in' an aw-ful
Str.
lot,
p
f
34
Str.
and I ought-n't bet a-gin a frog so ed-u-cat-ed.
p
f

Molto vivace
Str.
ff
But
35
a gam-bler's got to gam-ble, got to take the long-est
pp
pp
8
shot.
So
p cresc.
36
mp
I'll make you an of - fer, put up your
f
f
mf

p rit.
Str.
mon-ey and I'll match
pp
Quasi tempo di allegro (𝅗𝅥. = 76)
to Stranger p
37
Lu.
Aw - ful free with your cash!
Str.
it.
pp leggiero
sempre stacc.
Lu.
Watch it, you might save some to buy a girl a pres- ent.
p dolce
Stranger (aside to Lulu)
p
38
Str.
Eve-ry lit - tle thing in it's own time, don't get im -

Lu.
Is that a prom-ise? Well, a girl would kind-a like to know.
Str.
pa - tient. May - be so.
cresc.
Guitar Player (to the Crapshooters)
marc.
G.Pl.
Them out - land - ers think - in' how smart they are!
Str.
Don't you fret, Sug - ar,
mp
cresc.
39
1st Crapshooter
mp
1st Cr.
Think he'll take us all on?
Uncle Henry
p
U.H.
We'll stump 'im!
p
Str.
don't get im - pa - tient, don't get im - pa - tient,
p

Smiley comes rushing in, out of breath, mud up to his knees.

Sm.
Had to wade through a lot o' slime,
but I found you, I found you a
41
p dim.
Lu.
Show us, Smi-ley, let us see 'im!
Sm.
frog.
1st Cr.
Show us, Smi-ley, show us!
giggles
G.Pl.
Looks right peak-ed!
2nd Cr.
Show us, Smi-ley, show us!
giggles
p leggiero

42
1st Cr.
mf espress.
Don't com - pare with Dan - 'l!
Tweak it!
U.H.
mf espress.
Don't com - pare with Dan - 'l!
G.Pl.
mf espress.
Don't com - pare with Dan - 'l!
2nd Cr.
mf espress.
Don't com - pare with Dan - 'l!
Will he jump?
mp
p
Lu.
f
Git a - way!
1st Cr.
espress.
Don't com - pare with Dan - 'l!
U.H.
espress.
Don't com - pare with Dan - 'l!
G.Pl.
espress.
Don't com - pare with Dan - 'l!
2nd Cr.
espress.
Don't com - pare with Dan - 'l!
p
mp

43
Lu.
Sm.
U.H.
2nd Cr.
Str.
1st Cr.
G.Pl.
pp stacc.
No mo-lest-in'!
mp
No mo-lest-in'! It ain't sport-in'! It ain't
mf
p legato
Nope, it
Make it jump
with dignity
Tweak-in' we don't al-low.
p sub.
It ain't sport-in'! No mo-lest-in' the chal-leng-er now!
sport-in'! No mo-lest-in'!
pp
Tweak it! Tweak it! Tweak it!
don't com-pare with Dan-iel!
p legato
Don't com-pare with Dan-iel!
Make it jump! Make it jump! Make it jump!

44
1st Cr.
U.H.
G.Pl.
2nd Cr.
Don't com - pare with Dan - iel!
Don't com - pare with Dan - iel!
Don't com - pare with Dan - iel!
Don't com - pare with Dan - iel!
dim.
dim.
dim.
dim.
sempre dim.
8

45
pp ♩. = 84–88
1st Cr.
U.H.
G.Pl.
2nd Cr.
Make your bets, gents,
Make 'em large or small,
J.H.
Make your bets, make your bets,

MOVE IT

1) N.B. Stage money must be gold.

47
Takes coins out of her purse
Lu.
knew which side I'm on.
Sm.
mf
Dan - 'l can't lose!
1st Cr.
f
Doub-le mine, Stran-ger!
to Lulu
U.H.
f
Turn-in' on Dan-'l, Lu? Hard to for-
G.Pl.
burn-in' his pock-ets!
f
Doub-le mine!
mf
Stakes are
2nd. Cr.
mf
Stakes are high!
Str.
said, cash on the line.
Sure will!
p

to Uncle Henry
48
Lu.
Well, it's his jack and a girl's got-ta live! Got to
Sm.
Can't lose! I say
1st Cr.
to Lulu
Bet on Dan-'l, Lu,
U.H.
give!
G.Pl.
high! Climb-in' clean up to the sky!
2nd Cr.
An-oth-er twen-ty!
Str.
Why not? And

Lu.
— choose sides real care - ful now!
Sm.
Dan - 'l can't lose!
1st Cr.
come on. Dan - 'l Web-ster
G.Pl.
nasty mf
Some - thing
2nd Cr.
Dan - 'l Web-ster
Str.
twen-ty more for the la - dy!
p
49
1st Cr.
un - de - feat - ed, Give 'im chal-lenge, he 'll meet it!
G.Pl.
here 'pears might - y shad - y!
2nd Cr.
un - de - feat - ed, Give 'im chal-lenge, he 'll meet it!

Sm.
mf
cresc.
Dan - 'l Web - ster
1st Cr.
cresc.
Un - de - feat - ed, un - de - feat - ed,
U.H.
mf
Dan - 'l Web - ster
G.Pl.
No one listens to him
mf
cresc.
Dan - 'l
2nd Cr.
He - 'll meet it, he - 'll
Str.
mf cresc.
Your pet will
TENORS
T
mf cresc.
Dan - 'l Web - ster
BASSES
B
mf cresc.
Dan - 'l
mf
cresc.

50
Sm.
un - de - feat - ed.
1st Cr.
un - de - feat - ed.
U.H.
un - de - feat - ed.
G.Pl.
un - de - feat - ed.
2nd Cr.
beat it, he - 'll meet it, de - feat it.
Str.
be de - feat - ed.
T
un - de - feat - ed.
B
un - de - feat - ed.

mf cresc.
Lu.
Wish I knew who'll
Sm.
Bring an - y
1st Cr.
Bring up an - y
U.H.
Bring up an - y
G.Pl.
Bring up
2nd Cr.
Bring up an - y
Str.
My frog will
SOPRANOS
f cresc.
S
Bring up an - y
ALTOS
f cresc.
A
Bring an - y
TENORS
f cresc.
T
Bring up an - y
BASSES
f cresc.
B
Bring an - y
f

ff
Lu.
be de - feat -
Sm.
frog, he'll beat
1st Cr.
frog, he'll meet it and
U.H.
frog, he'll meet it and beat it, de -
G.Pl.
an - y frog,
2nd Cr.
frog, bring an - y frog, he - 'll
Str.
eas - 'ly beat
S
frog, he'll beat
A
frog, he'll beat
T
frog, he'll beat
B
frog, he'll beat

51
Lu.
ed.
Sm.
it, he'll meet it, he'll beat it,
1st Cr.
beat it, he'll meet it, he'll beat it,
U.H.
feat it, he'll meet it, he'll beat it,
G.Pl.
he'll beat it, de - feat it, he'll
2nd Cr.
meet it and beat it, de - feat it, he'll
Str.
it.
S
it.
A
it.
T
it.
B
it.
8
ff

Lu.
Sm.
de - feat it.
f
Now then, Stran-ger,
1st Cr.
de - feat it.
U.H.
de - feat it.
G.Pl.
meet it, de - feat it.
2nd Cr.
meet it, de - feat it.
Str.
S
A
T
B
8
3
3

52
Molto agitato (𝅗𝅥. = 96)
He takes Daniel out of his box.
He and Stranger make ready for the contest.
Sm.
if you're read - y, set your frog
p
sfp
53
a - long-side Dan - 'l, fore - paws
sfp
sf
2
e - ven. When I give the word, You poke 'im.
sf
sf
2
2
54
Ready-y, set, one, two, three,
sffp
cresc.

1) slang: *hoists, lifts.*

56
Sm.
1st Cr.
U.H.
G.Pl.
2nd Cr.
pp
Jump, jump, Dan-'l!
1 2 3 4 1 2 3 4
57
Jump, jump, Dan - 'l,
1 2 3 4 1 2

Sm.
1st Cr.
U.H.
G.Pl.
2nd Cr.
jump!
jump!
jump!
jump!
jump!
3 4 1 2 3 4
58
sfp
Jump!
sfp
Jump!
stacc.
Don't let that
stacc.
Don't let that oth - er frog show you up,
stacc.
Don't let that oth - er frog, don't let that oth - er frog show you up!
stacc.
Don't let that oth - er frog show you up, don't let 'im
1 2 3 4 5

stacc.
59
Sm.
Don't let that oth-er frog show you up!
Jump!
1st Cr.
oth-er frog show you up!
Jump!
U.H.
show you up!
Jump!
G. Pl.
Jump!
2nd Cr.
show you up!
Jump!
6
7
8
1
2
3
4
5
Timidly
Lu.
Don't let 'em down, Dan'l!
pp
6
7
8

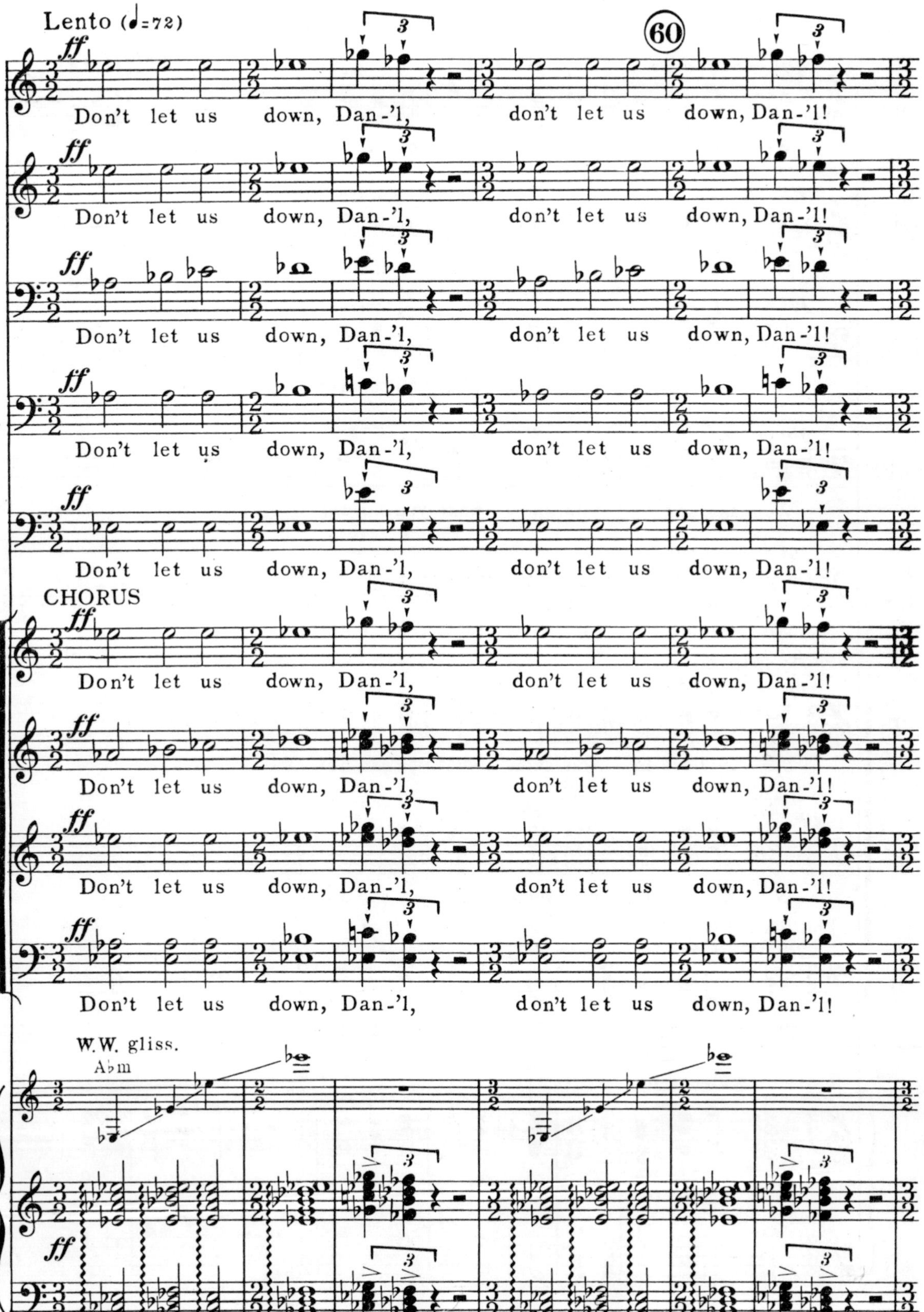

Lento (♩=72)
60
Sm.
Don't let us down, Dan-'l, don't let us down, Dan-'l!
1st Cr.
Don't let us down, Dan-'l, don't let us down, Dan-'l!
U.H.
Don't let us down, Dan-'l, don't let us down, Dan-'l!
G.Pl.
Don't let us down, Dan-'l, don't let us down, Dan-'l!
2nd Cr.
Don't let us down, Dan-'l, don't let us down, Dan-'l!
CHORUS
S
Don't let us down, Dan-'l, don't let us down, Dan-'l!
A
Don't let us down, Dan-'l, don't let us down, Dan-'l!
T
Don't let us down, Dan-'l, don't let us down, Dan-'l!
B
Don't let us down, Dan-'l, don't let us down, Dan-'l!
W.W. gliss.
A♭m

Daniel looks pitiful.
Sm.
1st Cr.
U.H.
G.Pl.
2nd Cr.
TENORS
T
1st BASSES
B
2nd BASSES
B
pp f espr. p
We be-lieve in you, show what you can do!
We be-lieve in you, show what you can do!
We be-lieve in you, show what you can do!
We be-lieve in you, show what you can do!
We _ be-lieve in you, show _ what you can do!
We be-lieve in you, show what you can do!
We be-lieve in you, show what you can do!
We _ be-lieve in you, show _ what you can do!
dolce espr.
p
dolce
poco rit.

Stranger pockets all the money Uncle Henry has been guarding, hands a twenty to Lulu. Everybody concedes Daniel's defeat.

FINALE

Allegretto (♩ = 76)
Piano
pp
p senza espr., ma dolce
sempre legato
62
pp almost whispered
Sm.
Un - hap - py day for Cal - a - ve - ras,
1st Cr.
Un - hap - py day for Cal - a - ve - ras,
U. H.
Un - hap - py day for Cal - a - ve - ras,
Our he - ro has struck out, He was the
mp poco marc.
G. Pl.
He was the
2nd Cr.
He was the

Lu.
mp
He's lost the jumping bout.
Sm.
p
pride of Cal-a-ve-ras, Oh
1st Cr.
pride of Cal-a-ve-ras, He's lost the jumping bout.
U.H.
pride of Cal-a-ve-ras, He's lost the jump-ing bout.
G.Pl.
pride of Cal-a-ve-ras, He's lost the jump-ing bout.
2nd Cr.
pride of Cal-a-ve-ras, He's lost the jump-ing bout.
63
Sm.
p molto
Oh!
1st Cr.
p molto
Oh!
U.H.
mf
Oh mis-for-tune, Oh dis-hon-or, Dan'l Web-ster lost the bout.
G.Pl.
p molto
Oh!
2nd Cr.
p molto
Oh!

U.H.
Str.
Aside
It might be smart to kind-a get an
p stacc.
Lu.
Un - hap - py day for Cal - a - ve - ras,
Sm.
Un - hap - py day for Cal - a - ve - ras,
1st Cr.
Un - hap - py day for Cal - a - ve - ras,
U.H.
Un - hap - py day for Cal - a - ve - ras,
G.Pl.
Un - hap - py day for Cal - a - ve - ras,
2nd Cr.
Un - hap - py day for Cal - a - ve - ras,
Str.
ear - ly start.
S
Un - hap - py day for Cal - a - ve - ras,
A
Un - hap - py day for Cal - a - ve - ras,
T
Un - hap - py day for Cal - a - ve - ras,
B
Un - hap - py day for Cal - a - ve - ras,
cresc.
p sub.

64
Lu.
Sm.
1st Cr.
U.H.
G.Pl.
2nd Cr.
S
A
T
B
mf
f
p legg.
Oh cru - el blow to all of us.
cresc.
p sub.

Half tender, half mocking
Lu.
Why, Dan-'l still keeps try-in', He sure looks like he's dy - in'.
Str.
That frog is good for nut-tin'!
legato
Aside to Stranger
p legg.
rit.
I'd kind-a like to put my lot in with a gen-tle-man like you.
Sm.
p
Oh!
UH.
p
Can't tell what frogs will do!
pp
L.H.
cresc. molto
rit.

65
a tempo
Lu.
Oh,
Sm.
Oh day of woe, Oh cru-el blow,
1st Cr.
Oh day of woe, Oh cru-el blow,
U.H.
Oh day of woe, Oh Oh
G.Pl.
Oh day of woe, Oh Oh
2nd Cr.
Oh day of woe, Oh cru-el blow,
Str.
With all this cash it might be smart to kind-a get an ear-ly start,
f a tempo
stacc.

Lu.
Oh, all is woe.
Sm.
All is lost, all is woe.
1st Cr.
All is lost, all is woe.
U.H.
All is lost, Oh, all is woe.
G.Pl.
All is lost, Oh, all is woe.
2nd Cr.
All is lost, Oh, all is woe.
Str.
to kind-a get an ear - ly start.
cresc.

Lu.
Un - hap - py day for Cal - a - ve - ras, un - hap - py
Sm.
Un - hap - py hour, un -
1st Cr.
Un - hap - py hour,
U.H.
Un - hap - py day for Cal - a - ve - ras, Oh cru - el
G.Pl.
Un - hap - py day for Cal - a - ve - ras,
2nd Cr.
Un - hap - py day for Cal - a - ve - ras,
Str.
Their glo - ry has a - bat - ed, their pride sure
CHORUS
S
Un - hap - py day for Cal - a - ve - ras, un - hap - py
A
Un - hap - py hour, un -
T
Un - hap - py day for Cal - a - ve - ras, Oh cru - el
B
Un - hap - py day for Cal - a - ve - ras,

66
Lu.
day for us, cru-el blow to all of us,
Sm.
hap - py day, Oh cru - el blow to all of us,
1st Cr.
cru - el blow to all of us,
U.H.
blow, cru - el blow to all of us,
G.Pl.
Oh cru - el blow to all of us,
2nd Cr.
Oh cru - el blow to all of us,
Str.
is de - flat - ed.
S
day for us, cru-el blow to all of us,
A
hap - py day, Oh cru - el blow to all of us,
T
blow, cru - el blow to all of us,
B
Oh cru - el blow to all of us,
p
mp
mf
p sub.

Lu.
Sm.
1st Cr.
U.H.
G.Pl.
2nd Cr.
S
A
T
B
f
p legg.
Oh day of woe for Cal-a-ve-ras.
cresc.
p sub.

Guitar Player exits slowly; everybody seems to disperse.
p legato e con sentimento
67
Stranger
p
poco rit.
Str.
Friends, I must be on my way,
pp
Bows deeply, hat off.
smorz.
Str.
let me bid you good day, good day! ______
ppp
Stranger exits
Poco più lento (♩= 63)
Lulu Simply
Lu.
Come, Smiley, have a snort;
it'll do you good.
ppp
pp

Daniel decidedly isn't feeling well.
Lulu
Lu.
Smiley
Sm.
He's
Hey, look it!
What in tar-na-tion!
68
ppp
p
pp
Tempo di allegretto (♩ = 76)
sick.
Smiley
What could be ail - in' him?
You,
p
He picks Daniel up.
Turns him upside down.
Dan-'l!
Why, blame my cats if he don't weigh five pound!
cresc.
cresc.
Daniel vomits buckshot.
ff
Crapshooters dash out.
A tremendous uproar is heard behind stage. Chairs and tables are heard being kicked about. Everybody is shouting.
Fellers! Bring that four-flusher 'round!
69
f

Everybody is back on stage. They surround the Stranger. Two of the men have their guns trained on him. Firm hands have him by the collar, and he is being propelled by knees in the backside.

70
Sm.
mp cresc.
bout that frog, — so you don't see no p'ints a-bout that frog that's
1st Cr
bout that frog? —
U.H.
mp cresc.
bout that frog, — so you don't see no p'ints a-bout that frog that's
G. Pl.
bout that frog? —
2nd Cr.
mp cresc.
bout that frog, — so you don't see no p'ints a-bout that frog that's
TENORS
T
mp cresc.
bout that frog, — so you don't see no p'ints a-bout that frog that's
1st BASSES
B
bout that frog? —
2nd BASSES
B
mp cresc.
bout that frog, — so you don't see no p'ints a-bout that frog that's
sf p f p cresc.

Sm.
f
bet-ter than an-y oth-er frog?
1st Cr.
f
No, none, none at all, no, none, none at
U.H.
f
bet-ter than an-y oth-er frog?
G.Pl.
f
No, none, none at all, no, none, none at
2nd Cr.
f
bet-ter than an-y oth-er frog? None, none at all, no, none, none at
SOPRANOS
S
f
No, none, none at all, no, none, none at
ALTOS
A
f
No, none, none at all, no, none, none at
TENORS
T
f
bet-ter than an-y oth-er frog?
1st BASSES
B
f
No, none, none at all, no, none, none at
2nd BASSES
B
f
bet-ter than an-y oth-er frog? None, none at all, no, none, none at
f

71
Lu.
You put your mon-ey
Sm.
You put your mon-ey
1st Cr.
all.
You put your mon-ey
U.H.
You put your mon-ey
G.Pl.
all.
You put your mon-ey
2nd Cr.
all.
You put your mon-ey
S
all.
You put your mon-ey
A
all.
You put your mon-ey
T
You put your mon-ey
BASSES
B
all.
You put your mon-ey
p
ff
f

Lu.
mf
on an-y oth-er frog, on
Sm.
mp cresc.
on an-y oth-er frog, you put your mon-ey on
1st Cr.
on an-y oth-er frog,
U.H.
mp cresc.
on an-y oth-er frog, you put your mon-ey on
G.Pl.
on an-y oth-er frog,
2nd Cr.
mp cresc.
on an-y oth-er frog, you put your mon-ey on
S
mf
on an-y oth-er frog, on
A
mp cresc.
on an-y oth-er frog, you put your mon-ey on
T
on an-y oth-er frog,
B
mp cresc.
on an-y oth-er frog, you put your mon-ey on
p

Lu.
cresc.
f
an-y oth-er frog, lay odds on it too, would-n't you? Don't hear you
Sm.
cresc.
f
an-y oth-er frog, lay odds on it too, would-n't you? Don't hear you
1st Cr.
f
would-n't you? Don't hear you
U.H.
cresc.
f
an-y oth-er frog, lay odds on it too, would-n't you? Don't hear you
G.Pl.
mf cresc.
f
lay odds on it too, would-n't you? Don't hear you
2nd Cr.
cresc.
f
an-y oth-er frog, lay odds on it too, would-n't you? Don't hear you
S
cresc.
f
an-y oth-er frog, lay odds on it too, would-n't you? Don't hear you
A
f
an-y oth-er frog, lay odds on it too, would-n't you? Don't hear you
T
f
would-n't you? Don't hear you
B
f
an-y oth-er frog, lay odds on it too, would-n't you? Don't hear you
cresc.
f

72
Lu.
brag-gin' now; what you got to say for your-self?
Sm.
brag-gin' now; what you got to say for your-self?
1st Cr.
brag-gin' now; what you got to say for your-self?
U.H.
brag-gin' now; don't hear you brag-gin' now!
G.Pl.
ff
brag-gin' now; don't hear you brag-gin' now! Fork o - ver!
2nd Cr.
brag-gin' now; don't hear you brag-gin' now!
S
brag-gin' now; what you got to say for your-self?
A
brag-gin' now; what you got to say for your-self?
T
brag-gin' now; what you got to say for your-self?
B
brag-gin' now; don't hear you brag-gin' now!
They shake the Stranger: money rolls out of his pocket.
p
sf

Frantic, almost whining
ff
Str.
I'm just a — stran - ger here, I — had no —
f
legato
f
Lu.
Here a girl thinks she's get - tin a break!
3
Str.
stake, I had no stake, I'm
73
Str.
Pleading
just a — stran - ger — here. Miss Lulu, you under stand ?
pp subito, cresc.
They close in on the Stranger,
Lulu in front, leading the attack.
f dim.
p

Lu
p
If you show your face in this town a - gain
Sm
p
If you show your face in this town a - gain
1st Cr.
p
If you show your face in this town a - gain
UH
p
If you show your face in this town a - gain
GPl
p
If you show your face in this town a - gain
2nd Cr.
p
If you show your face in this town a - gain
S
p
If you show your face in this town a - gain
A
p
If you show your face in this town a - gain
T
p
If you show your face in this town a - gain
B
p
If you show your face in this town a - gain

74
Lu.
mp cresc.
we'll tar and feath - er you and draw and quar - ter you and
Sm.
mp cresc.
we'll tar and feath - er you and draw and quar - ter you and
1st Cr.
mp cresc.
we'll draw and quar - ter you and
U.H.
mp cresc.
we'll tar and feath - er you and draw and quar - ter you and
G.Pl.
2nd Cr.
mp cresc.
we'll tar and feath - er you and draw and quar - ter you and
S
mp cresc.
we'll tar and feath - er you and draw and quar - ter you and
A
mp cresc.
we'll tar and feath - er you and draw and quar - ter you and
T
mp cresc.
we'll draw and quar - ter you and
B
mp cresc.
we'll tar and feath - er you and draw and quar - ter you and
p cresc.

Lu.
string you up and ride you on a rail, we'll
Sm.
string you up and ride you on a rail,
1st Cr.
ride you on a rail and truss you up like a Christ-mas goose,
U.H.
string you up and ride you on a rail,
G.Pl.
and truss you up like a Christ-mas goose,
2nd Cr.
and truss you up like a Christ-mas goose,
S
string you up and ride you on a rail.
A
string you up and ride you on a rail.
T
ride you on a rail and truss you up like a Christ-mas goose,
B
and truss you up like a Christ-mas goose,
f

p stacc.
Lu.
doub-le tar and feath-er you and string you up and quar-ter you and
p stacc.
Sm.
doub-le tar and feath-er you and string you up and quar-ter you and
p stacc.
U.H.
we'll
pp legg.
Lu.
doub-le tar and feath-er you and string you up and quar-ter you and
Sm.
doub-le tar and feath-er you and string you up and quar-ter you and
p stacc.
1st Cr.
we'll
U.H.
doub-le tar and feath-er you and string you up and quar-ter you and
p stacc.
G.Pl.
we'll
p stacc.
2nd Cr.
we'll

75
cresc.
Lu.
feath - er you and quar - ter you and feath - er you and quar - ter you and
Sm.
feath - er you and quar - ter you and feath - er you and quar - ter you and
1st Cr.
feath - er you and quar - ter you and feath - er you and quar - ter you and
U.H.
feath - er you and quar - ter you and feath - er you and quar - ter you and
G.Pl.
feath - er you and quar - ter you and feath - er you and quar - ter you and
2nd Cr.
feath - er you and quar - ter you and feath - er you and quar - ter you and
Lu.
feath - er you and quar - ter you and feath - er you and quar - ter you and
Sm.
feath - er you and quar - ter you and feath - er you and quar - ter you and
1st Cr.
feath - er you and quar - ter you and feath - er you and quar - ter you and
U.H.
feath - er you and quar - ter you and feath - er you and quar - ter you and
G.Pl.
feath - er you and quar - ter you and feath - er you and quar - ter you and
2nd Cr.
feath - er you and quar - ter you and feath - er you and quar - ter you and

Lu.
next time, next time it - 'll be the noose!
Sm.
next time, next time it - 'll be the noose!
1st Cr.
next time, next time it - 'll be the noose!
U.H.
next time, next time it - 'll be the noose!
G.Pl.
next time, next time it - 'll be the noose!
2nd Cr.
next time, next time it - 'll be the noose!
S
Next time, next time it - 'll be the noose!
A
Next time, next time it - 'll be the noose!
T
Next time, next time it - 'll be the noose!
B
Next time, next time it - 'll be the noose!

76
Più sostenuto (𝅗𝅥 = 69)
Lu.
Here's to Dan - iel the frog, here's to
Sm.
Here's to Dan - iel the frog, here's to
1st Cr.
Here's to Dan - iel the frog, here's to
Kicks Stranger out.
U.H.
Now, git! Here's to Dan - iel the frog, here's to
G.Pl.
Here's to Dan - iel the frog, here's to
2nd Cr.
Here's to Dan - iel the frog, here's to
S
Here's to Dan - iel the frog, here's to
A
Here's to Dan - iel the frog, here's to
T
Here's to Dan - iel the frog, here's to
B
Here's to Dan - iel the frog, here's to
ff
rit.

77
a tempo
rit.
molto sost.
p cresc.
f
Lu.
Dan - iel the frog, here's to Dan - iel the frog
Sm.
Dan - iel the frog, here's to Dan - iel the frog
1st Cr.
Dan - iel the frog, here's to Dan - iel the frog, the
U.H.
Dan - iel the frog, here's to Dan - iel
G.Pl.
Dan - iel the frog, here's to Dan - iel
2nd Cr.
Dan - iel the frog, here's to Dan - iel
S
Dan - iel the frog, here's to Dan - iel the frog
A
Dan - iel the frog, here's to Dan - iel the frog
T
Dan - iel the frog, here's to Dan - iel the frog, the
B
Dan - iel the frog, here's to Dan - iel
p rit.

Vivace (𝅗𝅥 = 138-152)
Lu.
p sub.
ff
of Cal-a-ve-ras Coun-ty.
Sm.
fff
still cham-pion of Cal-a-ve-ras Coun-ty.
1st Cr.
p sub.
ff
frog of Cal-a-ve-ras Coun-ty.
U.H.
f
p sub.
ff
the frog of Cal-a-ve-ras Coun-ty.
G.Pl.
f
p sub.
ff
the frog of Cal-a-ve-ras Coun-ty.
2nd Cr.
f
p sub.
ff
the frog of Cal-a-ve-ras Coun-ty.
S
p sub.
ff
of Cal-a-ve-ras Coun-ty.
A
p sub.
ff
of Cal-a-ve-ras Coun-ty.
T
p sub.
ff
frog of Cal-a-ve-ras Coun-ty.
B
f
p sub.
ff
the frog of Cal-a-ve-ras Coun-ty.
cresc.
sf
ff

[1]For television or movie production, Daniel gathers himself up for a great jump, swells as he takes a gargantuan breath, and sails right into the camera, looming larger and larger until he fills the screen.

Lulu's Song *

LUKAS FOSS
(1953)

* Added in the Venice Festival performance, 1952 Written for Anne Brown (Lulu)

ne-ver been a-ble to stand the thought of a wo - man-less man. It
makes me so lone-some my-self, So lone-some my - self, I do
for him all that I can.
rit.
p
When I was a slip of a

girl My folks used to warn me and say: Your
3
heart is as big as a house, No sense let-ting in ev-'ry
stray.
pp
I've let in all sorts in my
tr
time, There's some who will say it's a sin, And
f
8
pp

still when a lone-ly man asks,
When a lone-ly man
asks, I like to in-vite him right in.
rit.
a tempo
poco rit.
Lulu exits
You just wait here.
pp

CARL FISCHER

MUSIC